London: City

GW01454860

LONDON IS A VIBRANT CITY, with somethi... its people offer such a cosmopolita... ways that it has been described as ... ...ation. The capital of the United Kingdom, London was al... ...historic capital of an empire which once encompassed a quarter of the world's population, and this imperial past is the background to much of the splendour of the city's heritage today.

London has grown and developed naturally over the years – it was never planned in the manner, say, of Paris or New York, and its heart is a delightful confusion of winding alleyways and small, secret courtyards. Tidier patterns of squares, crescents and terraces may be seen, and modern development has raised the distinctive blocks and high towers of the financial centre. Yet almost one third of London is open space, and it is easy to dodge out of a busy street to relax in one of the city's famous parks.

From its double-decker buses to its guardsmen in their red tunics, London is richly steeped in tradition and pageantry. This is celebrated in forms as diverse as the colourful Costermonger's Harvest Festival, when the street vendors get together with their Pearly Kings and Queens, to the solemn dignity of the State Opening of Parliament, attended by the Sovereign, Queen Elizabeth I. Dr Johnson's famous tag holds just as true today: *'When a man is tired of London, he is tired of life; for there is in London all that life can afford.'*

ABOVE The central panel of the beautiful and unusual Queen Elizabeth Gate, on Hyde Park, one of London's newest royal monuments. Kings and queens are celebrated all over the capital, from the dramatic statue of Boudicca by Westminster Bridge to the Victoria and Albert Museum in Kensington, its foundation stone laid by Queen Victoria herself in 1899.

2

ABOVE London's first section of underground railway was opened in 1906, and now it is impossible to imagine the city without its network. The train service, known as the Tube, is now one of the world's biggest underground railways, operating every day except Christmas Day and serving over 270 stations. During the bombing in World War II, many Londoners took refuge in the comparative safety offered by the Underground stations.

Finding Your Way

LONDON, BISECTED from east to west by the River Thames, can be bewildering for its sheer size. However, its centre on the north bank, where the major visitor attractions may be seen, is not difficult to explore.

The City, to the east of the main centre, is London's financial heart, and here you will find the Tower of London and St Paul's. The West End is the smart quarter of London in which to shop and be entertained – this is the elegant world of Mayfair, of Harrods and theatreland, of Soho and also the best restaurants and hotels. The East End, beyond Tower Bridge, was traditionally the area of docklands and the poor working-class, the home of Cockneys and rhyming slang, and the polar opposite of the West End – but rebuilding and redevelopment are transforming this area, and here you will find attractions like the Design Museum and HMS *Belfast*.

London has so much to offer that it is impossible to see it all in one visit. A guided bus tour is a great way to get your bearings, or take a boat trip on the river.

The following is a list of top attractions to help you plan your visit.

LONDON'S TOP ATTRACTIONS

Houses of Parliament
Westminster Abbey
St Paul's Cathedral
Madame Tussaud's
London Planetarium
Tower of London
Natural History Museum
Museum of the Moving Image
National Gallery
Museum of London

*A*BOVE *A view across the River Thames to the Houses of Parliament and Westminster Bridge. The Thames is still a busy thoroughfare for boats of all sizes.*

*B*ELOW *The familiar bright red double-decker is an essential feature of the capital, and on a summer's day there can be no better way of seeing the city than from an open topped bus.*

*A*BOVE *In recent years London's famous black taxi cabs have started to appear in all the colours of the rainbow, and all-over advertising has become another feature. London cabbies must pass very strict tests and examinations before they are allowed onto the streets, and their knowledge of the city can be extraordinary.*

ENTRY TO THE TRAITORS' GATE

*A*BOVE The central keep of the Tower of London dominates the view from across the river.

*L*EFT This medieval illustration shows how little the Tower, surrounded by walls up to 15ft (4.5m) thick, has changed.

*R*IGHT Built around 1411, the Guildhall is a remarkable survivor of both the Great Fire and the Blitz. Hung with banners of the major livery companies, it was used in the past for state trials.

Historic London

LONDON OWES ITS EXISTENCE to chance and the building of a bridge. The Emperor Claudius had intended that Colchester, in Essex, should be the capital of Roman Britain, and that is where the Roman invasion force headed in AD43 after landing near the site of today's Richborough, in Kent. To reach Colchester, the Romans had to cross the Thames, constructing a wooden bridge not far from the site of the present London Bridge. Soon the main focus of the new Roman road network, Londinium developed into a thriving settlement and port. Rebuilt after an attack by Boudicca's Iceni tribe, it became the capital of Britannia around AD100. London's early history is excellently told at the Museum of London, and remains of the Roman wall of AD200 may still be seen in the museum grounds.

The period following the withdrawal of Roman troops from Britain in AD410 is one of the most intriguing in history, because so little is known about it. However, we do know that the first churches were built in London in the 7th century, if not before, and archaeological finds suggest that the port of London continued to prosper, exporting wool and cloth.

London as we know it today began to develop during the reign of Edward the Confessor, who came to the throne in 1042. He devoted his income to a magnificent new abbey church at Westminster, building a royal palace alongside it. This marked a decisive shift away from the old Roman city, and from that time London consisted of two distinct parts: the royal centre around Westminster and the commercial centre in the City.

The importance of Westminster was confirmed when William I, the Norman Conqueror, was crowned King of England in the abbey. The White Tower, the old heart of the Tower of London, was built as the new monarch's principal fortress.

A huge number of immigrant workers began to settle in London, occupying the area around Cheapside – whole streets were devoted to particular crafts or products, as names such as Bread Street, Poultry Lane and Goldsmiths Row still recall.

TOP *This head of Mithras, the Persian god of light, was discovered along with the remains of a Roman temple in Walbrook in 1954, as new offices were being constructed. The temple, used until AD350, was carefully rebuilt and preserved.*

ABOVE *Yeomen Warders, or Beefeaters as they are known, guard the Tower. Their distinctive uniforms date back to Tudor times.*

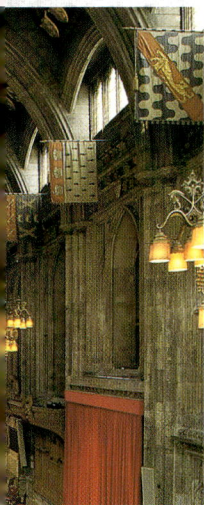

The Great Fire

LONDON GREW APACE in the 16th century, until it was home to one in 20 people living in England. The city was seriously overcrowded, but planning laws in 1592 to prohibit new building within a three-mile radius had little effect. No area was rougher than Southwark, where Shakespeare's Globe Theatre was built in 1598–9, beside the brothels, taverns, bearpits and cockpits to which the city's apprentices flocked for entertainment.

The City of London sided with Parliament in the Civil War, and its opposition to Charles I was a potent factor in his defeat. The King paid with his head, in Whitehall. At the Restoration of the Monarchy in 1660, Charles II rode in triumph through a rejoicing London. Two dramatic events soon followed: the Great Plague, in which around 100,000 people died, and the Great Fire of London.

On the night of 2 September 1666, a baker's shop in Pudding Lane caught fire – the Monument was later erected to mark the spot. The Lord Mayor was apparently alerted that night, but reportedly said the fire was so trivial that 'a woman might piss it out'. That this was a serious misjudgement became clear the next morning, when the great diarist Samuel Pepys was horrified to learn that 300 houses were already destroyed, and that nobody was attempting to quench the flames. The fire raged for three days, and nearly every building in the City was burnt down – 13,200 houses, 44 guildhalls and 87 churches. Remarkably, only nine people lost their lives.

The task of rebuilding – in brick, stone and tile this time – fell to Sir Christopher Wren, whose masterpiece among many fine buildings is St Paul's Cathedral. This heralded the start of a building boom in the capital that would last for 100 years.

In 1694 a group of London merchants combined to form the Bank of England, and the City's pre-eminence as a financial centre was assured.

ABOVE A contemporary illustration shows the devastation of the Great Fire on the overcrowded city.

BELOW The Monument was erected in 1671 to commemorate the Fire.

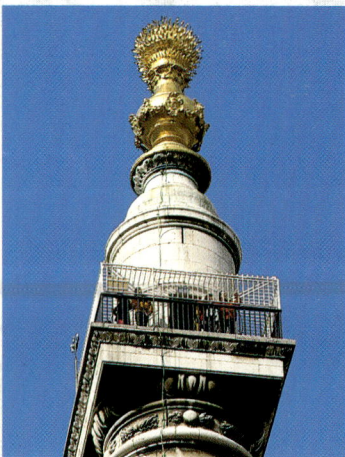

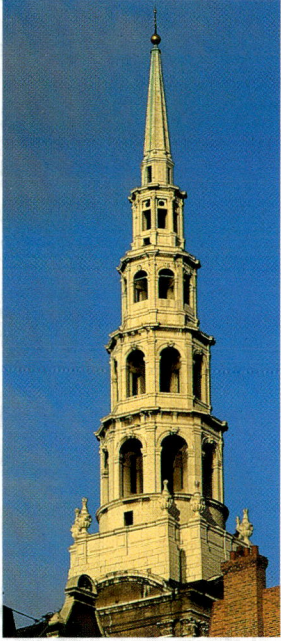

ABOVE St Bride's church in Fleet Street was built in 1684 by Sir Christopher Wren, although the lovely 'wedding cake' spire was not added until 1701.

ABOVE This sign marks London's most famous public house, for centuries the haunt of writers, including Dr Johnson and G K Chesterton.

TOP AND LEFT St Paul's Cathedral is a lasting monument to its designer, Wren. The dome houses a bell, Great Paul, and inside is the famous Whispering Gallery.

RIGHT Named after the then Prince Regent, Regent Street sweeps in a splendid curve through the heart of the West End, from Piccadilly where Eros (above) reigns.

BELOW The Royal Albert Hall, built in 1851, is home to the popular annual Promenade Concerts.

Capital of an Empire

IF THE REBUILT GEORGIAN LONDON was an affluent and civilised place of coffee-houses, sedan chairs and luxury shops, it was also crude, dangerous and filthy, with open sewers running through the streets and the air thick with smoke from coal fires.

In a major exercise in town planning, early in the 19th century, the architect John Nash planned Regent Street as a grand boulevard of graceful terraces, running north from the centre to Regent's Park. At the same time London's docks were extending busily down river, and new bridges were being built over the Thames. Multitudes of the poor, meanwhile, were crammed into appalling slums, in a world brought vividly to life in the novels of Charles Dickens. The arrival of the railways in the 1840s meant cheaper transport, and workers were able to move further out of the city centre, gradually swallowing up villages like Hampstead and Highgate.

Victorian London was the world's largest city, the capital of the world's foremost nation, and the centre from which the biggest empire in history was ruled. The power, wealth and bounding self-confidence of this age are reflected in many of today's familiar landmarks, from the Victoria and Albert Museum and the Houses of Parliament to the Royal Albert Hall and Nelson's Column.

While damage to the city in World War I was comparatively light, saturation bombing during the Blitz, from 1940, was a different matter. People sheltered in the underground stations, thousands of homes were destroyed – in one night alone, 28 incendiary bombs fell on St Paul's – and over 20,000 people lost their lives.

The capital sprang back to life with the Festival of Britain in 1951, and the Clean Air Act of 1956 made London the first smokeless zone in Britain and banished the old 'pea-souper' smogs. In recent times, the port has declined along with shipping worldwide, but campaigns to clean up the river have brought fish and wildlife back into the city.

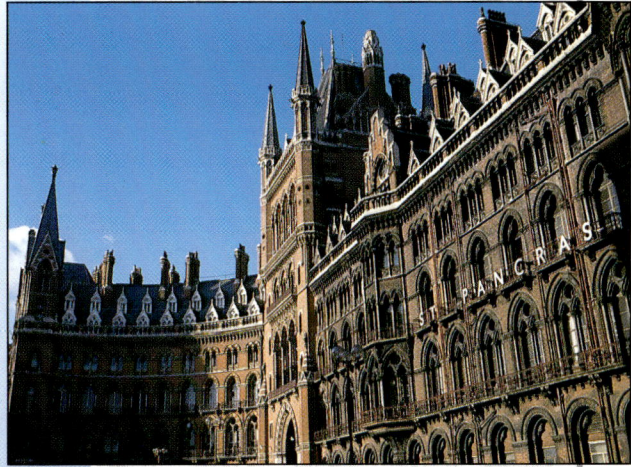

RIGHT Blue plaques mark the homes of famous London inhabitants.

TOP AND BELOW A fine example of Victorian Gothic, and the 1950s South Bank complex.

ABOVE A royal procession is one of the great sights of London, and the Chelsea Pensioners (BELOW), old soldiers living out their days at the Royal Hospital, often take part, dressed in their 17th-century uniform of red frock-coat and tricorn hat.

Royal London

FROM ITS PAGEANTRY to its palaces, London is bound up with royalty. For more than 400 years the principal royal residence was the Palace of Westminster – the law courts met here, Charles I was tried and condemned in the hall in 1649, and it was here that coronation banquets were held on the accession of each monarch until King George IV's time. Every coronation since 1066 has been celebrated in Westminster Abbey, and in 1947 Queen Elizabeth II, then Princess Elizabeth, married Lt Philip Mountbatten here in a glittering ceremony.

Kensington Palace was a favourite royal residence in the 18th century, and Queen Victoria was actually born at the house – the Prince of Wales still has apartments there. St James's Palace has not been used extensively as a royal home since the early 19th century; Marlborough House and Clarence House, in St James's, have both been used by royalty.

With Queen Victoria's accession to the throne, the focus moved firmly to Buckingham Palace, where the Royal Family still live today – 'above the shop', as Prince Philip remarked, for most of the 600 rooms are offices for staff. Royal garden parties are held in the grounds, and the Changing of the Guard is one of the capital's most popular tourist attractions. The royal standard flying from the roof is the sign that the Queen is in residence, and on state occasions the Royal Family appear together on the palace balcony, to acknowledge the crowds of well-wishers who gather round the Victoria Memorial.

Another of London's great spectacles is provided on state occasions, when the Queen and her mounted guard process down the Mall – the wide avenue which leads from Buckingham Palace – along the north side of St James's Park, and into Trafalgar Square.

*T*OP *The imposing east wing of Buckingham Palace is mainly devoted to offices – the Royal Family's rooms are on the quieter north side, facing the gardens.*

*A*BOVE *Guardsmen in their tall bearskin helmets are a familiar sight in london, whether on sentry duty or taking part in a state occasion such as Trooping the Colour (RIGHT), on Horseguards Parade.*

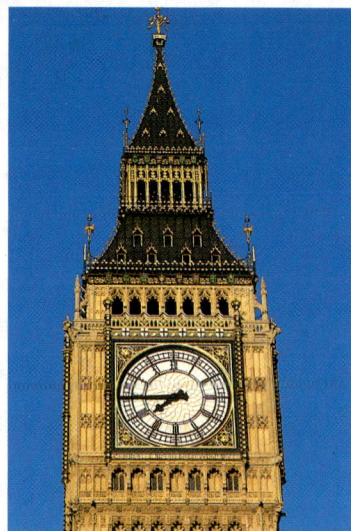

*T*OP AND LEFT *The high clock tower of the Houses of Parliament contains probably the most famous, and certainly one of the most accurate, public clocks in the world. The hands are 14ft (4.2m) and 9ft (2.7m) long. Although the tower is often called Big Ben, the name actually applies to the huge bell inside the clock itself.*

*A*BOVE *A London 'bobby' on guard outside Britain's best-known address: 10 Downing Street, home of the Prime Minister.*

Seat of Government

THE NEWLY-CLEANED STONEWORK of the Houses of Parliament dominates Parliament Square, although perhaps the best views are to be had across the river, from the far side of Westminster Bridge. Edward the Confessor built the Palace of Westminster on this site in 1049 and successive monarchs used it as their main London residence until 1529. Parliament first met in the Chapter House of Westminster Abbey, but moved to the Palace of Westminster in 1547, where it has met ever since. The present remarkable building, a Gothic extravaganza by Barry and Pugin, was opened in 1852. A flag flying from the big square Victoria Tower by day, and a light shining from the clock tower of Big Ben by night, indicate when Parliament is sitting.

The fine twin towers of Westminster Abbey, completed in 1745, are one of the latest additions to a building begun by Edward the Confessor 700 years before, and added to by successive monarchs. It is here, on an ancient wooden throne, that monarchs are crowned, and here that they are buried, along with national heroes, warriors and poets. The tombs of Queen Elizabeth and her cousin Mary, Queen of Scots, are among the first to be seen, and the tomb and chapel of Henry VII are among the greatest funerary monuments in Europe. The Chapel of Edward the Confessor lies at the heart of this great church, and the simple Tomb of the Unknown Soldier is just inside the main entrance. His body was buried here in soil brought over from the battlefields of France on 11 November 1920. The so-called 'Poets' Corner' is in the south transept, and here the names of the great form a roll call of British history, art and science, with memorials to Shakespeare, Sir Isaac Newton, Handel and many others.

Parliament Square was laid out in the 19th century to provide a garden setting with panoramic views of the Houses of Parliament and Westminster Abbey. The numerous statues in the square are of famous statesmen, including Sir Winston Churchill, and Field-Marshal Smuts, a staunch South African ally in World War II. The statue of Abraham Lincoln was presented by the American people in 1920.

ABOVE AND BELOW The Church of Great Britain, Westminster Abbey is a 'royal peculiar' rather than a cathedral, with the sovereign, not a bishop as its head. Inside, monuments include one to Shakespeare.

WILLIAM SHAKESPEARE 1564 - 1616
BURIED AT STRATFORD-ON-AVON

A Walk Around London

The Jubilee Walk, of which this is part, was inaugurated in 1977 to commemorate the silver jubilee of Queen Elizabeth's accession to the throne. Waymarked by special crown symbols, the route is occasionally liable to change for road or building work.

1 LEICESTER SQUARE

This famous square takes its name from Leicester House, a mansion built here in the 17th century, but long since gone.

2 NATIONAL GALLERY AND NATIONAL PORTRAIT GALLERY

Housed in the National Gallery is one of the finest and most extensive collections of masterpieces in the world. The adjoining National Portrait Gallery has the world's most comprehensive survey of historical personalities.

3 TRAFALGAR SQUARE

Laid out in memory of Lord Nelson, Trafalgar Square was designed in 1829-41 by Sir Charles Barry.

4 CARLTON HOUSE TERRACE

John Nash designed this dignified group of buildings as part of his architectural scheme for Regent Street.

5 DUKE OF YORK STEPS AND COLUMN

This 112ft granite pillar commemorates the second son of George III. The cost of its erection is supposed to have been defrayed by stopping a day's pay from every man in the army.

6 THE MALL

The Mall was originally laid out in 1660-2 as part of Charles II's scheme for St James's Park. It was transformed into a processional way in 1910.

7 ST JAMES'S PARK

Although it is comparatively small, St James's is perhaps the

ROUTE DIRECTIONS

Follow west side of Leicester Sq (1) and cross into St Martin's St. At the end follow footpath alongside the National Gallery (2) bearing right to Whitcomb St. Turn left, then left again into Pall Mall East. Cross over and continue along west side of Trafalgar Sqare (3). Cross Cockspur St into Spring Gardens, passing through the iron gates and descending the steps to the Mall, keeping Admiralty Arch on left. Turn right, passing Carlton House Terrace (4), the Mall Galleries, and the Duke of York Steps and Column (5) on right. Cross the Mall (6), with a distant view of Buckingham Palace on right, and enter St James's Park (7). Bear left to pass the lake, then right and shortly turn left to leave the park. Turn right along Horse Guards Rd, and at the end turn left into Great George St passing Storey's Gate on right. At Parliament Sqare (8) turn right, then left along south side of sqare and St Margaret's Church (9), with Westminster Abbey (10) to right. Turn right into St Margaret St and continue into Abingdon St, passing Houses of Parliament (11) on left and the Jewel Tower (12) on right. Just beyond Great College St cross at pedestrian crossing and turn left to return along Abingdon St. Shortly turn right into Victoria Tower Gardens, and at the Burghers of Calais statue bear right and follow the riverside pathway. At end ascend steps out of park and turn left to cross Lambeth Bridge. On far side turn left and descend steps on to Albert Embankment, with Lambeth Palace and St Mary's Church (13) to right. Walk along the Albert Embankment (14) with Westminster Bridge (15) ahead. Ascend steps and cross Westminster Bridge Rd by the South Bank Lion (16). Descend steps and continue along Embankment, passing County Hall (17) on right. Keep on the South Bank (18) and then enter Jubilee Gardens, to finish the walk at the Silver Jubilee Pedestal in Jubilee Gardens (19).

SILVER JUBILEE WALKWAY 1977

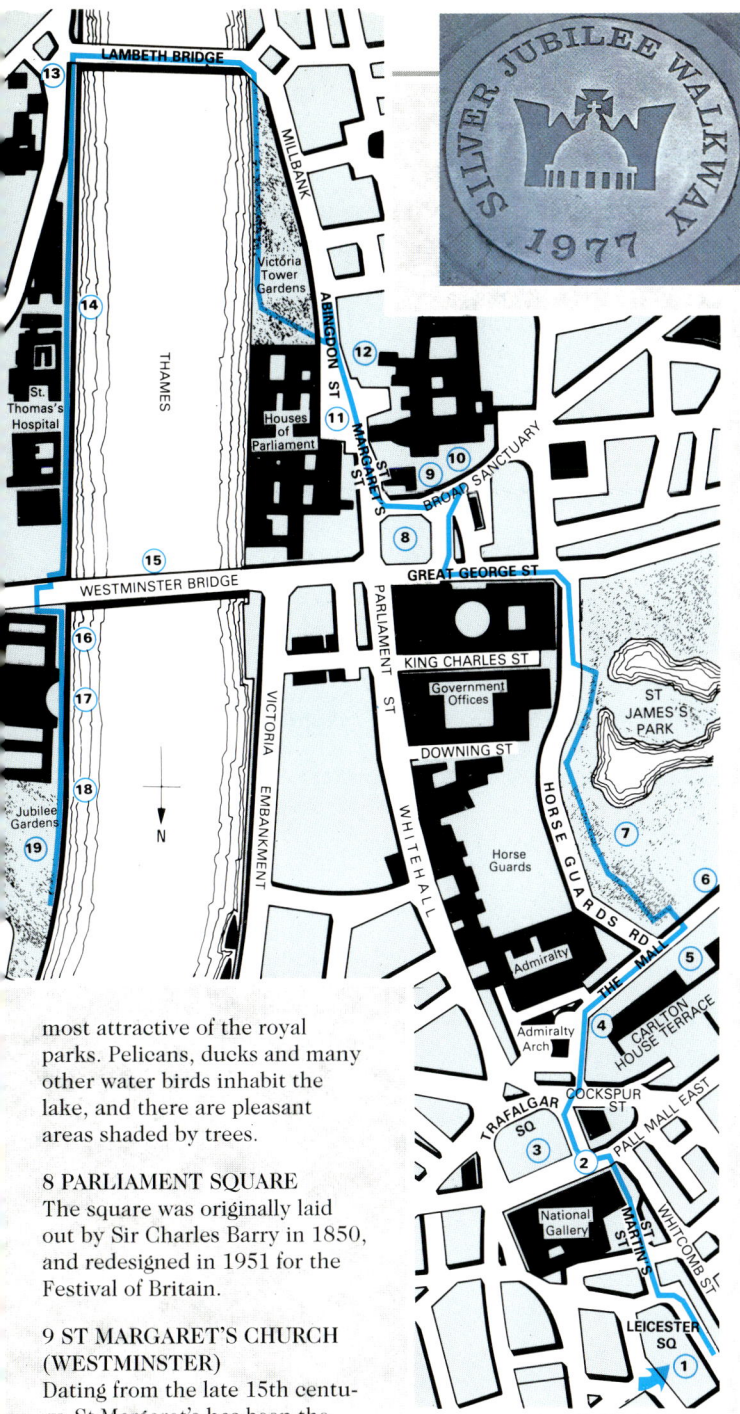

12 THE JEWEL TOWER
This inconspicuous moated tower is a survival of the medieval Palace of Westminster, built to house the monarch's personal treasure.

13 LAMBETH PALACE AND ST MARY'S CHURCH
Much of this historic structure, which has been the London residence of the Archbishop of Canterbury for 700 years, was rebuilt during the 19th century. The most interesting parts are the Lollards' Tower and the Gatehouse, both 15th-century, and the 13th-century Chapel Crypt. Adjoining the south gateway is the former church of St Mary, now restored as a Museum of Garden History in memory of John Tradescant, Charles I's gardener. Captain Bligh, of *Bounty* fame, is buried here.

14 ALBERT EMBANKMENT
The earliest section of walkway (1868) was built as a river defence for St Thomas's Hospital.

15 WESTMINSTER BRIDGE
The present bridge was designed by Thomas Page and completed in 1862, replacing a stone bridge of 1750.

16 SOUTH BANK LION
The lion at the foot of Westminster Bridge previously surmounted the Lion Brewery, which was demolished to build the Royal Festival Hall.

17 COUNTY HALL
Originally erected in 1912-32, the colonnaded front facing the Thames is 750ft long.

18 SOUTH BANK
The walkway between County Hall and Hungerford Bridge is lined with London plane trees.

19 JUBILEE GARDENS
These gardens were laid out to celebrate Queen Elizabeth II's Silver Jubilee in 1977.

most attractive of the royal parks. Pelicans, ducks and many other water birds inhabit the lake, and there are pleasant areas shaded by trees.

8 PARLIAMENT SQUARE
The square was originally laid out by Sir Charles Barry in 1850, and redesigned in 1951 for the Festival of Britain.

9 ST MARGARET'S CHURCH (WESTMINSTER)
Dating from the late 15th century, St Margaret's has been the official church of the House of Commons since 1614.

10 WESTMINSTER ABBEY
A church has stood on this site since at least as early as Saxon times – see page 13.

11 THE HOUSES OF PARLIAMENT
The present building was designed by Sir Charles Barry and Augustus Pugin and built in 1836-60.

ABOVE Despite its 18th-century appearance, the delightful musical clock above the door of Fortnum & Mason was installed in 1964.

BELOW The open-air market at Portobello Road is a great place for bargain hunters, and best known for its own particular combination of bric-à-brac and genuine antiques.

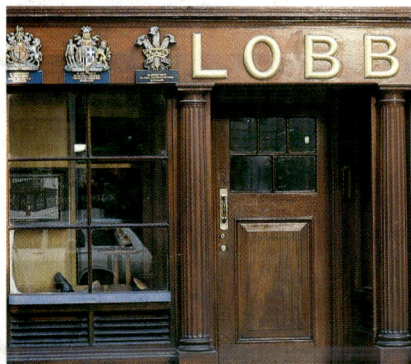

TOP Harrods, the legendary department store, serves around 35,000 customers a day. By contrast, this apparently modest little cobbler's shop in St James's (ABOVE) makes boots for royalty.

London Shopping

LONDON BOASTS ONE OF THE WORLD'S richest and most varied collections of shops and markets, selling goods of every type, quality and price. The smartest, best-known shops are concentrated in the West End, around Bond Street, St James's Street, Piccadilly, Jermyn Street, Regent Street, Oxford Street, Covent Garden, Brompton Road and Kensington High Street. Some streets have attracted shops of the same sort: Charing Cross is known for bookshops, Bond Street for picture dealers, jewellers and high fashion shops, and Kensington High Street for its starry cluster of antique shops. A discreet coat of arms above a shop door is the sign of royal patronage.

Harrods of Knightsbridge is the largest department store in Europe, and needs no introduction. Selfridges, on Oxford Street and second only to Harrods in size, was the proud creation of American tycoon George Selfridge, back in 1909. On Regent Street, Garrard & Co are the Crown jewellers, and Hamleys, which claims to be the world's biggest toyshop, is a five-storey paradise for children. Just off Piccadilly, the Burlington Arcade has some of the most elegant small shops in the city.

Fortnum & Mason on Piccadilly, with its appealing clock, is another great London institution. Staff on the ground floor still wear formal morning clothes, but in other ways the shop is innovative – its buyers, for example, were the first to place an order in 1886 with a young man called H J Heinz. Founded in 1707 by Hugh Mason, a grocer, and William Fortnum, a footman at the court of Queen Anne, the shop's association with royalty has continued over the centuries. There is probably no luxury food that is not stocked here, and the hampers are legendary.

Adding colour, humour and lively cut-and-thrust to the London scene, street markets and street vendors are vigorous survivors of London's long tradition of open-air trading. Of the markets, Portobello Road is best known for antiques, Petticoat Lane for its Cockney atmosphere, and Columbia Road for its plants.

*T*OP *The smart Burlington Arcade preserves some ancient laws – patrons may not run, sing, whistle or open an umbrella beneath its august roof. Liberty's stylish emporium (ABOVE) is another popular centre.*

ABOVE The collection at the National Gallery, seen here across the fountains in Trafalgar Square, has been growing steadily since around 1824.

BELOW Trafalgar Square has something to appeal to everybody, from the infamous pigeons to the cooling fountains. The graceful architecture of St-Martin-in-the-Fields, facing the square (RIGHT), marks the parish church of the Royal Family, built between 1721 and 1726.

London Landmarks

A majestic Landseer lion

TRAFALGAR SQUARE is the setting for one of London's best loved landmarks, Nelson's Column, which stands over 184ft (55m) high. The four bronze relief panels on the base of the monument were cast from French cannon captured at the Battle of Trafalgar, and the great lions are by Sir Edwin Landseer.

A bronze plaque just behind the equestrian statue of Charles I marks the official centre of London, in the square which is, in effect, the village green of the city – here people congregate spontaneously on New Year's Eve, for political demonstrations, or simply to feed the innumerable pigeons which make it their home. Every Christmas an immense fir tree, presented by the Norwegians in thanks for British help in World War II, is erected in the square – becoming the bright focus for carol singers.

The National Gallery, fronting imposingly onto Trafalgar Square, houses a magnificent collection of 'Old Masters', with over 2,000 paintings by artists from Giotto to Picasso. The National Portrait Gallery, another fine collection sometimes described as the nation's family album, is tucked round behind it, in St Martin's Place.

The Tate Gallery, on Millbank, houses two more great national collections: of British art from the 16th century, including works by J M Turner and the Pre-Raphaelites, and of modern, international art. Works from widely differing periods and artists are juxtaposed here to provoke and challenge the viewer, and while the result is often controversial, this remains one of London's most popular galleries.

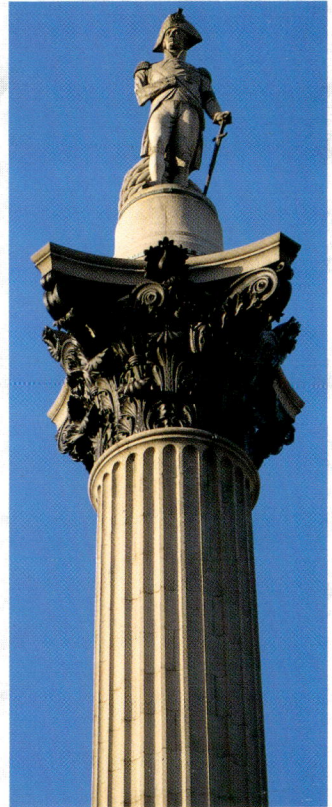

ABOVE Nelson, 17ft (5m) high, dominates the square named after his most famous victory.

19

BELOW The Tate is famous for its controversial exhibitions of modern art – this is by Max Ernst.

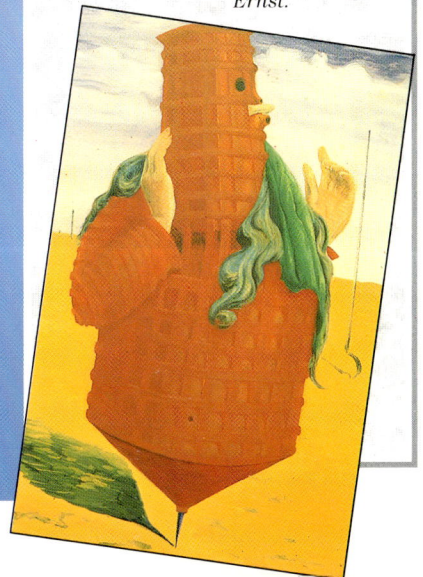

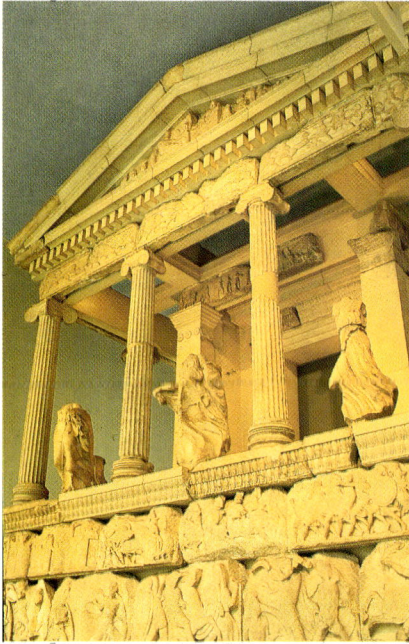

ABOVE *The Nereid Monument, from Xanthos in Asia Minor, is among the outstanding collection of Greek and Roman antiquities at the British Museum, a centre for scholarship and research.*

LEFT *Recreating the mood of the musical 'My Fair Lady' at Covent Garden, the site of the old flower market.*

COVENT GARDEN is another lively centre, developed on the site of the old vegetable market. In 1980 the central market buildings and those surrounding the Piazza were restored and adapted to house boutiques and cafés, with market stalls in the arcade selling antiques, crafts, toys, jewellery and clothing. The Punch and Judy pub is a reminder that the first ever Punch and Judy puppet show was held here in 1662. There is still a light-hearted tradition of outdoor entertainment, from buskers to street theatre.

Two more famous London pubs are the Prospect of Whitby in Wapping Wall, once a haunt of Samuel Pepys and artists such as Turner and Whistler, who came to paint the river views, and The George, near London Bridge, which features in several novels by Dickens. The original building on this site, which was frequented by Shakespeare, burned down in 1676, and was rebuilt in the 17th century as a replica of the medieval hostelry, with wooden galleries overlooking a central courtyard.

Shaftesbury Avenue is just one of London's streets famous for its theatres, which are scattered all around this central area. The Barbican, near the Museum of London, is the capital's newest arts centre, with concert halls to rival the Royal Festival Hall on the South Bank.

A recent addition to the South Bank complex is the Museum of the Moving Image, a lively hands-on tribute to the world of film and TV. The British Museum takes a more traditional approach, but its collections of archaeological treasure include everything from the Sutton Hoo Treasure to one of the richest collections of Egyptian art to be seen anywhere in the world.

*L*EFT *Piccadilly Circus, once known as the 'hub of the Empire', is brought to life by its brilliant advertising hordings and the familiar statue of Eros.*

*B*ELOW *One of London's famous theatre venues.*

*A*BOVE *One of the city's favourite landmarks, Madame Tussaud's famous waxworks display has been going strong since 1835, with old favourites such as the Chamber of Horrors, and new attractions such as a time-ride through London.*

On the River

ABOVE Canary Wharf, a towering monument to the building optimism of the 1980s, now dominates the south London skyline.

BELOW The polished line of the Greenwich Meridian, outside the Old Royal Observatory.

ST KATHERINE DOCK, just east of Tower Bridge, was built by the great engineer Thomas Telford, and forms part of old Docklands – the three basins of the dock are home now to a variety of modern craft and historic ships. Dominated by the mighty tower of Canary Wharf, 800ft (234m) high and the tallest building in Britain, modern Docklands offers a lively contrast. Once an overgrown wilderness of disused docks and crumbling warehouses, a gleaming city of the future has been developed, with a remarkable combination of enlightened planning, new architecture (some splendid, some distinctly idiosyncratic) and thoughtful preservation of old buildings.

Five miles below Tower Bridge the Thames leads gracefully to Greenwich on the south shore, and many visitors choose to arrive in style by riverboat. One of the first sights is of the sailing ship *Cutty Sark*, one of the last and fastest tea-clippers, now anchored in a dry dock near Greenwich Pier. The symmetrical wings of the Royal Naval College line the waterfront here – originally designed by Sir Christopher Wren as a home for disabled and aged seamen, it retained the view from the river of the Queen's House, glimpsed at the centre.

Once simply a riverside village, Greenwich retains its lovely park (the London Marathon starts here) and a charming mixture of stately historic buildings, Georgian houses, Victorian terraces and delightful little shops. Looking down from the Old Royal Observatory today, it is easy to picture Greenwich's Tudor past, when Greenwich Palace stood near the Queen's House. Here Henry VIII was born in 1491 and here, too, Queen Elizabeth I spent the happiest hours of her childhood.

Britain's history as a seafaring nation is brought vividly to life in the National Maritime Museum, which includes two galleries devoted to Lord Nelson, one of Britain's greatest admirals.

LEFT The Old Royal Observatory was built to establish latitude and help with stellar navigation. The Cutty Sark (ABOVE) houses a museum of ships' figureheads.

BELOW Lit up at night, the Gothic turrets of Tower Bridge span the Thames. The central bascules can be raised in minutes to allow ships to pass underneath.

*T*OP *Historic Windsor Castle is set in the extensive grounds of Windsor Great Park. Hampton Court (RIGHT) is one of the oldest royal palaces.*

*A*BOVE *The Royal Air Force Museum at Hendon has a remarkable collection of aircraft on display.*

Around London

WITHIN EASY REACH, north of the city centre, Hampstead is another favourite London 'village' with a distinctive character. To the north lie 800 acres (324ha) of woods and open spaces – Hampstead Heath – and the Vale of the Heath, a romantically named valley, Parliament Hill Fields and Highgate Ponds all contribute to Hampstead's aura of rural charm. Many of the well-preserved houses are open to the public, including that of the poet Keats. Kenwood House is one of London's finest stately homes, and open-air concerts are held by the lake here in summer. Highgate Cemetery is an unusual attraction, remarkable for the range of its funerary architecture, and for the number of famous people buried there, including Charles Dickens and George Eliot.

To the east, beyond Greenwich, the futuristic Thames Barrier was built across the river to protect a sinking London from potential flooding.

Up-river again, and south-west of the city, the Thames flows on through Richmond and past the mellow red-brick palace of Hampton Court, built in the 16th century by Cardinal Wolsey but later confiscated and enlarged by Henry VIII. Highlights here include the massive hammerbeam roof of the Great Hall, and the famous maze in the park.

Further to the west lies Windsor Castle, a favourite royal residence, set in the vast acreage of Windsor Great Park. Parts of the castle were destroyed by fire in 1992, but restoration work costing upwards of £30 million will repair much of the damage, and most of the castle was not affected. The impressive state apartments are hung with works from the royal collections, and a star attraction is Queen Mary's Doll's House – the furnishings are designed at one-twelfth lifesize, the plumbing and lighting really work, and famous artists and authors have contributed miniature paintings and hand-written books.

TOP Red and fallow deer roam free in Richmond Park, enclosed by Charles I in 1637 as a royal hunting ground.

ABOVE The memorial to Karl Marx is one of the most famous at Highgate Cemetery.

Calendar of Events

There are hundreds of events in London every year, some very big, like the Lord Mayor's Show, and some tiny, like the Ceremony of the Lilies and Roses. The most famous events – royal pageants such as Trooping the Colour – can attract huge crowds.

JANUARY

Lord Mayor of Westminster's New Year's Day Parade
Marching bands, floats and performers parade from Piccadilly to Hyde Park Corner, culminating in a firework display.

30 January: Charles I Commemoration Ceremony
Members of the Society of King Charles the Martyr and the Royal Stuart Society commemorate the execution of Charles I in 1649, with a procession from St-Martin-in-the-Fields to the equestrian statue of the King in Trafalgar Square.

FEBRUARY

Chinese New Year
London's Chinatown is decorated for this lively event, and a procession led by a 'lion' weaves through the area around Gerrard St, receiving gifts from shops.

The Clown Service, Holy Trinity Church, Dalton
A memorial to Joseph Grimaldi, one of the most famous clowns of all time, is here, and the service is attended by clowns in full costume.

MARCH

Oxford and Cambridge Boat Race
A contest over four miles, from Putney to Mortlake, between two crews of eight rowers representing the universities of Oxford and Cambridge – one of the most famous sporting events in the world.

Oranges & Lemons Children's Service, St Clement Dane's Church, Strand
A special service to mark the restoration of the church bells, well-known from the children's nursery rhyme 'Oranges and Lemons'; children attending from the primary school each receive an orange and a lemon.

APRIL

Spring Flower Show
A colourful affair, held at the Royal Horticultural Society Halls, Vincent Square.

MAY

Ceremony of the Lilies and Roses, Tower of London
On 21 May, representatives of Eton College and King's College, Cambridge, both founded by Henry VI, join in a ceremony marking the anniversary of his murder, laying lilies from Eton and roses from King's on the spot where he died in 1471.

Chelsea Flower Show
The great event of the gardening year, held since 1913 in the grounds of the Royal Hospital, Chelsea.

London Marathon
Thousands of runners join in this good-humoured race from Greenwich to Westminster, many raising money for charity.

JUNE

Trooping the Colour
Held on the Queen's official birthday, the second Saturday of June, this is the most spectacular military display of the year. The Queen travels down the Mall from Buckingham Palace to Horse Guards Parade, where the Brigade of Guards and the Household Cavalry await her. Her Majesty takes the salute, and this is followed by a display of marching and the 'trooping' or carrying the colours of a selected regiment.

Lawn Tennis Championships, Wimbledon
Usually running from June into July, this is the most famous tennis tournament in the world.

JULY

Swan Upping
Held around the last Monday of July, between London Bridge and Henley, this ceremony marks the inspection by the Queen's Swan Keeper and wardens of the Vintners' and Dyers' Livery Companies, in full traditional costume, of all the swans on the river, establishing ownership of swans and cygnets.

AUGUST

Notting Hill Carnival
Held in the Portobello Road area, this is one of London's noisiest, friendliest events, with a large contribution by the city's Caribbean population.

SEPTEMBER

Last Night of the Proms, Royal Albert Hall
The last of the famous series of Henry Wood Promenade Concerts, celebrated in a traditional dating back to 1895.

OCTOBER

State Opening of Parliament
In one of London's most colourful pageants, the Queen travels to the Houses of Parliament, where, in full ceremonial dress, she makes a speech from the throne in the House of Lords, outlining the government's proposed legislation for the new parliamentary session.

NOVEMBER

London to Brighton Veteran Car Run

Cars built between 1895 and 1904 take part in this, leaving from Hyde Park Corner on the first Sunday of the month. The first organised run was in 1933 – all the cars are beautifully cared for, and many of the drivers and passengers dress in period costume.

Lord Mayor's Show

On the second Saturday, the new Lord Mayor publicly takes office, riding from the Guildhall to the Royal Courts of Justice in a gilt coach (usually displayed at the Museum of London), attended by

Pikemen and Musketeers in a colourful parade, the City's most spectacular showpiece.

DECEMBER

Christmas Tree and Carol Singing, Trafalgar Square

Every year a giant Christmas tree is donated to London by the people of Oslo, Norway; set in Trafalgar Square, it is the focal point for evening carol services from around 16 December.

*T*OP *The London Marathon;* *(*ABOVE*) Swan Upping ; (*LEFT*) the Lord Mayor's Show.*

LONDON 3-STAR SIGHTS

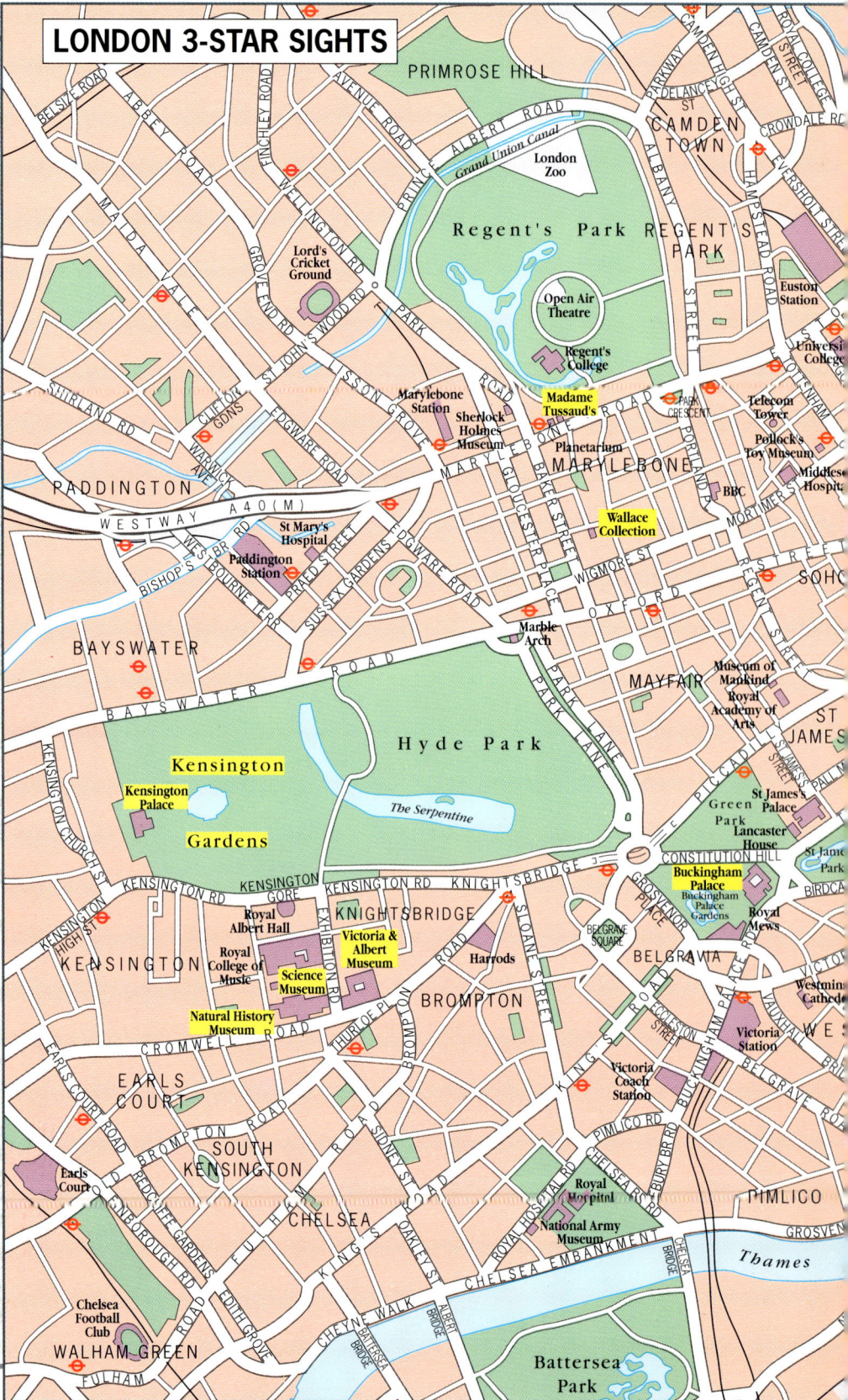

PRIMROSE HILL

BELSIZE ROAD

ABBEY ROAD

MAIDA VALE

FINCHLEY ROAD

AVENUE ROAD

ALBERT ROAD

PRINCE ALBERT ROAD

Grand Union Canal

CAMDEN HIGH ST

CAMDEN STREET

CROWDALE RD

DELANCEY ST

CAMDEN TOWN

ROYAL COLLEGE STREET

HAMPSTEAD STR

London Zoo

Regent's Park

REGENT'S PARK

Open Air Theatre

Regent's College

Euston Station

University College

GROVE END RD

ST JOHN'S WOOD RD

Lord's Cricket Ground

LISSON GROVE

PARK ROAD

ALBANY STREET

PORTLAND PLACE

Euston
Station

PARK CRESCENT

Telecom Tower

SHIRLAND RD

CLIFTON GDNS

EDGWARE ROAD

Marylebone Station

Sherlock Holmes Museum

Madame Tussaud's

MARYLEBONE ROAD

Planetarium

MARYLEBONE

Pollock's Toy Museum

BBC

MORTIMER ST

Middlesex Hospital

PADDINGTON

WESTWAY A40(M)

WARWICK

BISHOP'S BR RD

WEST BR RD

St Mary's Hospital

Paddington Station

PRAED STREET

SUSSEX GARDENS

BOURNE TERR

EDGWARE ROAD

GLOUCESTER PLACE

BAKER STREET

Wallace Collection

WIGMORE ST

OXFORD

SOHO

BAYSWATER

BAYSWATER ROAD

Marble Arch

PARK LANE

MAYFAIR

Museum of Mankind

Royal Academy of Arts

ST JAMES

The Serpentine

Hyde Park

PICCADILLY

Green Park

St James's Palace

KENSINGTON CHURCH ST

Kensington

Kensington Palace

Gardens

Lancaster House

CONSTITUTION HILL

St James Park

St James's Park

KENSINGTON HIGH ST

KENSINGTON RD

KENSINGTON GORE

KENSINGTON RD

KNIGHTSBRIDGE

GROSVENOR PLACE

Buckingham Palace

Buckingham Palace Gardens

Royal Mews

BIRDCA

KENSINGTON

Royal Albert Hall

Royal College of Music

EXHIBITION RD

Victoria & Albert Museum

Science Museum

KNIGHTSBRIDGE

SLOANE STREET

BELGRAVE SQUARE

Harrods

BELGRAVIA

Westminster Cathedral

VICTORIA

Natural History Museum

CROMWELL ROAD

THURLOE PL

BROMPTON ROAD

BROMPTON

Victoria Station

BELGRAVE RD

WE

EARLS COURT

EARLS COURT ROAD

BROMPTON ROAD

SIDNEY ST

SOUTH KENSINGTON

Victoria Coach Station

BUCKINGHAM PALACE RD

VICTOR

Earls Court

REDCLIFFE GARDENS

FULHAM ROAD

OAKLEY ST

KING'S ROAD

Royal Hospital

ROYAL HOSPITAL RD

PIMLICO RD

PIMLICO

GROSVEN

CHELSEA

National Army Museum

CHELSEA EMBANKMENT

CHELSEA BRIDGE

Thames

Chelsea Football Club

WALHAM GREEN

FULHAM

EDITH GROVE

CHEYNE WALK

BATTERSEA BRIDGE

ALBERT BRIDGE

Battersea Park